# Age of Innocence

# Age of Innocence

David C. Bellusci

RESOURCE *Publications* • Eugene, Oregon

AGE OF INNOCENCE

Copyright © 2020 David C. Bellusci. All rights reserved. Except for brief quotations in critical publications or reviews, no part of this book may be reproduced in any manner without prior written permission from the publisher. Write: Permissions, Wipf and Stock Publishers, 199 W. 8th Ave., Suite 3, Eugene, OR 97401.

Resource Publications
An Imprint of Wipf and Stock Publishers
199 W. 8th Ave., Suite 3
Eugene, OR 97401

www.wipfandstock.com

PAPERBACK ISBN: 978-1-7252-8027-4
HARDCOVER ISBN: 978-1-7252-8026-7
EBOOK ISBN: 978-1-7252-8028-1

Manufactured in the U.S.A.                    07/31/20

*In memory of my mother and father,
Rosa Montagano and Nicola Bellusci*

*Describe your sorrows and desires,
passing thoughts and the belief in some sort of beauty—
describe all these with loving, quiet sincerity, and use,
to express yourself, the things in your environment, the images
from your dreams, and the objects of your memory.*

—Rainer Maria Rilke,
Letters to a Young Poet

# Contents

*Acknowledgements* | ix

**I: Book of Nature** | 1

Angelic Park | 3
Meaning of Farm | 4
Silent Swings | 5
First Days of School | 6
Arithmetic Book | 8
Unmoved Cats | 9
Mother's Day in the Park | 10
River Melody | 12
Granville Island Blues | 14
Celtic Green | 15
Painted Window | 16
Stellar Dance | 18
Equine White | 19

**II: Course in Metaphysics** | 21

Bee-ing | 23
Aristotelian Morphology | 24
Reminiscing in Blue | 30
Heraclitus: Lessons at Dawn | 31
Saturday Morning | 32
Broken Glass or *Rethinking Kleist's "Das Zebrochne Krug"** | 34
Shattered Child | 35

Ember and Ash | 36
Autumn Lake | 37
Last Night | 38
You Sit on a Table | 39
Lost on the Tarmac | 40

**III: Cities and Fields** | 41

In Brackets | 43
Danger: Overhead Work | 44
Blvd. de Maisonneuve | 45
Western Tracks* | 46
Waking up between Continents | 48
Arkansas Weekend | 49
Rhoda's Tamales | 50
Altar of MonteAlbán* | 51
Septima | 52
Soaking Rwanda | 54
Tribute to Mandela | 55
Atlantic Desert, Southwest* | 57
Across the Sinai | 59
Gulf Windows | 60
Relics of Goa | 61
Bombay Lights | 62
Bollywood Moves | 64
Tea Ceremony | 65

## IVa: O r a n g e P o r t r a i t s | 67

Scent of Copenhagen | 69
La Haïtienne | 71
Donut Shop | 73
Carpenter in the Winter | 74
Sherbrooke Street | 75
Pigeon Lady | 79
Leather-Tapper | 80
Aufwiedersehen | 81
Father's Day at My Desk | 83
Mr. Penny | 85
Whatever Happened
 to Baby . . . ? | 87
Table for One—
 Two Years Later | 88
Again | 89

## Vb: CLINIC
### Doors/Recovery | 91

Appointment | 93
Emergency | 94
Admitted* | 96
December's Paradox | 98
Hiding MySelf | 100
It's Getting Dark | 102
Sounds in My Head | 103
Isolated | 105
Delirium or Delusion | 107
Tram I Won't Forget | 108
Morning from the Hospital | 109
Junction | 110
Silent Syllables | 111
Ecstasy* | 112

# Acknowledgements

I AM ESPECIALLY GRATEFUL to the late poet laureate, Pier Giorgio Di Cicco, whose poetry has been a source of inspiration for me. Meeting with Pier Giorgio in Toronto in the winter of 2004, he offered me words of encouragement that have kept me writing.

The late visual artist, Francesca L'Orfano, reminded me that art "is meant to be communicated." My many enriching conversations with Francesca on poetry and art directed me towards publication.

I am indebted to the poets and mentors who "formed" me in poetry, in particular, Allison Adelle Hedge Coke, Teri Grimm, and Lee Ann Roripaugh at the University of Nebraska. Their communication of the poetic craft and the page, punctuation and the word, have been the "metaphysical" foundation to my writing.

The Association of Italian-Canadian Writers have been a supportive group of creative writers that provided me with a forum to read my work, listen to fellow writers, and exchange ideas.

In the area of mental health and working in spiritual care, I am grateful for the guidance and friendship of Dr. Hannah Pytlak, Prof. John Morgan, and Rev. Ajith Varghese.

My family and friends, sisters and brothers, nephews and nieces, aunts and uncles, and godchildren, in Canada, Italy, USA, Nicaragua, Mexico, Finland, India, and Kenya, I am grateful for their presence in my life.

Thank you to my sister who has always been there for me . . .

# I

Book of Nature

# Angelic Park

Purple wings lined in gold silk,
Dominique glides, Francis and Michel
stop in a soundless flutter.

Firs pour pine needles on treetops;
I chew the cones, secretly.
A laurel for each of us drips
with carmel pistachios.

Sprinkling lavender and basil
on blueberries
we ascend through clouds . . .
flap on the shore.

Turquoise waves, emerald crystals,
shower us.
Like a magic wand—a spell—
that taps we fall, enchanted.

The horizon an orange ball opens,
eggs break, yoke and white
gently lick the night sky.

Moon craters point to Orion,
spaced stars dance frozen.

We position ourselves:
feathered flight launched.

## Meaning of Farm

Orange pumpkins
dot the farm.
Fence and gate, rust entrance,
peacocks appear. The narcissistic
males disappear head-up.
Sheep in a kraal,
or is that Afrikaans?
I am here for bacon and eggs,
and so is Mike.
He refuses to explain
what a "farm" is—*it's obvious*.
I know geese bite, their stare,
a warning. I still wonder why, "farm"?
Perhaps the smell of horse manure?
Or the dirty pig running loose?
The fourteen-year old waitress sits
with us—talks about her teachers.
We wave at her mom. She sat
in the usual third pew
on Friday night.
The farm helps me forget.
Birds that pray at sunrise
keep Mike company
or they may lose him.

## Silent Swings

We faced northern mountains
          I pulled back the seat and pushed
my cousin Isabelle,
          hands tight on the chains of her swing.
                  Her laugh, screams,
aiming for white clouds.

Breeze cuddles me,
          egrets pose their neckline
a storybook river surrounds us
I drink summer grass.

          Sea plane hums
into afternoon dandelions,
          birds pierce the turquoise.

She motions with her cotton fingers:
I find my tough boy strength.

          I jump onto my swing
          ceaseless pleasant rhythm.
Sudden force sends my body high,
          Isabelle laughs.

I wondered who catches us

          in heaven . . . ?

## First Days of School

September begins, crispy air,
        Indian summer stretches.

Months slip past . . . meditating
on the veranda,
        *what happened?*

Inhaling tobacco
        confused
        my holidays
eclipsed
by unexpected college studies.

That school uniform delighted
the family:
        navy blue trousers
        pastel shirt
        sweater and tie
complete with
Latin school crest:
        *Deum quaero.*

        *Friends, would I have any?*
        *What games would we play?*
        *Would they even like me.*

First day like a first date
        awkward
        shyly standing.

*Guys go for football and girls*
*for the guys,*

she reveals her unhidden motives,
while naive parents pay for religion.

Girls show off claims:
       *cool* to be seen with . . . *Someone,*
passion and impulses define truth:
flesh, smoke and keys.

How shallow it *all* seemed
       by eighteen.

I fled—shielded—I studied unharmed.

I dream of the sun unveiling
the course philosophers point to.

*Ideas:* mine—of sages—God's.

A galaxy of mystery: *Why here?*

September haunts me, and books
terrify:

I know an answer is carved . . .

## Arithmetic Book

In my Grade Two arithmetic book
only the picture page interested me.
Black numbers = equations
+ and − I ignored.
Sidewalk. Two green shrubs.
Perfect house: full page.
Perfect Yard. Door. Entrance.
Framed windows. Polka dot curtains.
A-shaped roof.
My mind jumped into the house,
to say:
This is my house.
One sidewalk.
One door.
One chimney.
Two shrubs.
Two windows.
Black lines defined my house.
I never solved the arithmetic problem
because houses do not contain numbers
and equations do not construct my world.
I discovered years later my house
belonged to Plato.

**Unmoved Cats**

Cool rain pours—
        morning warns, indoors-not-out

streets flush cars
wet sequence repeats.

From a bay window two cats stare
        at foolish busy-bodies
      carry briefcases, wear back-packs.

Puzzled felines aghast.

Human rationality confuses,

stretch out to understand
        sapien mechanics.

Mutual comfort reassured
knitted furs purr

        grey skies loom
        predictable waters patter.

Large window sealed by small frames
coated in drops dripping
condense the hum-drum day

          eyes stop blinking.

## Mother's Day in the Park

Silly-putty kids hang==from monkey bars
        sandy sight        to land on.
Parents reminisce
                chewing summer grass . . .

Beams of light hit green leaves
        white joy-bubbles rise==pop:
      shrieks imitate gulls.

Two Chinese boys at badminton:
        black hair reflects the sun.
Cream coloured t-shirts—brown trousers
        mom cheers==each son's victory!

Italians gather==*la famgilia* reunion:
      men barbecue sausage holding beer,
     gold-necklaced women spoon tomato sauce
on *penne*.        Cousins chase cousins.

Battery airplane lands in the dirt==
        controlled by a shirtless boy:
        jumps hysterically
        to maneuver his toy.

                Spotty refuses
to release==a blue frisbee, teased by the owner
to fetch the plastic . . .
        fearless three year-old
follows:
        trio entangle in beastly battle.

Spanish syllables roll==two round women
in Spandex and Adidas—push a baby buggy.
Their *hombre* arrives on roller blades—

wobbles ahead.

                       . . . Turquoise table cloth—
huge bowl of green salad & fresh salmon
cover our picnic table. Mamma's kerchief
neatly tucked—smiles, Mona Lisa-like.

## River Melody

Moonlight secrets touch morning sky
gracious birds migrate:
defined space.
Dawn paints lavender and orange.

Green figures hiss and sway
stretch along hidden banks
where chatty-tailed occupants
find shelter.

Self-focussed waters contemplate
their rhythmic splash:
eternal marries the infinite
envious sun ignored.

At nightfall silhouette marks men canoeing,
Mohawk chants:
soft sounds beat to rowers' paddle
island destined for dance rituals.

Gothic twin steeples announce God,
Atlantic charts a new river
cedars—maple—fleur de lis—
Crown imposes monumental victory.

Electrical lines—industrial smoke,
red and blue flags—modern glass art,
cement square blocks—
construction blasts create culture.

Semi-nude runners, clumsy
roller bladers, confident cyclists
chased by dogs snarling. Hand in hand,
assured lovers walk,
babies strapped in strollers.

Crane stands to conduct its symphony,
dandelion and heather accompany.

Thunderstorm interrupts:
concerto begins.

## Granville Island Blues

peaks dance . . . . . . .
—yachts tug . . . . . . . speed
. . . . . . . children . . . . . . . seagulls eye . . . . . . .
promenade on wet wood—shouts . . . . . . .
parents with strollers . . . . . . . couples in love
. . . . . . . ice cream cones—scoops—sorbet-to-taste
. . . . . . . board passengers transit
north shore—suburbia—shop . . . . . .

circumvent the island

. . . . . . . tiny crafts—short cruise

whistles blow . . . . . . . Vancouverites wave
island village in the city . . . . . . .
southern tourists—local bench bathers
happy dog strollers . . . . . . . aimlessly accompany
screech . . . . . . . cries—birds intrude
wasps intimidate—unsuspecting
. . . . . . . exotic foods—sweet-tasting snacks
railway tracks—Granville bridge
converge . . . . . . . piece of land . . . . . .

ripples . . . . . . . .

# Celtic Green

still
        green-filled days

stolen

            frozen
            leafless

       hibernal

snow painted branches

unveil scented thistle and cone

            emerald textures
            off prints

ice crystals
sprayed fir and pine

blanket layers sketch the horizon

clouds open

       silent distant dawn

       empty road

           as if waiting

## Painted Window

Blue-green brushes

        stroke my window
        Renoir's pastels impressions.

Navy-turquoise contrast by night
        Van Gogh's delirium.

Shape of pine etched on orange

skies cool,
evening scent

        starry flashes
        announce autumn—

Relentless winds howl at leaves

        scattered
        green yellow—abrupt hush.

Hills of the Haute Loire roll within,

        thoughts afar fuse, *now*

        thunder showers
        crack.

Indian summer traces the sun
deep gold orange

—drops of green pine—

   punctual glow

magic on my window
               forgetting the artist

        inside.

## Stellar Dance

        diamond lights        pulsate

thoughtful arrangement

on black satin        breathing glow

majestic spin

        I touch        their teasing rays

Verdi composes his seasonal notes—conducts
standing on Mont Blanc

        moon drops

violin   cello

        symphony performed

        dance of Venus

flat cosmic        rhythms

        transcendent

    steps

# Equine White

        winged horse
        traces
        starry sky

heavy breath
nostrils
        thick neck
                inclines

smooth back        invites

    icy currents
    light sparks
    full moon
        determined path

silhouette white horse
        glides
        freely, spheres possesses

unknown friend waits, longs

tastes the presence
        infinite
        enfleshed

        lead

to    delicious heavens
      Eternal harmony.

# II

## Course in Metaphysics

## Bee-ing

lace . . . . creature . . . . buzz
uncharted lines . . . . summer  sun  blaze
. . . . scented  spot . . . .

blue petals conceal . . . . sweet  juices  seized
  bumble  body  lands
  transmits      things

. . . . cherry blossoms  motorized search
  profit  exchange  rewards
taste exquisite

perfumes  in  sequence . . . . pull
like magnet
. . . . instinctive habits  repeat

  silk  textures layered
sensuous  signal sent . . . . dizzy  ecstasy

  golden  powder  black umbrellas
nectars drip . . . .

  gracious stop . . . .
    . . . . created  being

## Aristotelian Morphology

touch me
        occupy
        my space

=sacred presence
        fingers
        hands

stroke—caress
        my body
        in tingly sensation

and when i taste
            lingual activity

+ total tongue
        informs me what is desired/repulsed
        inches of tissue refined

shapes pain/pleasure:life/death
        gland un/hidden, relative to human corpus
        discrete demands of space and size

distant waves in low/high frequency
        spatio-temporal
        identifiable patterns—signalled contexts:

baby's cry, mamma's voice
        Robin sings, Laborador barks
        airplane hums beneath clouds

vocalic syllables sooth, gurgles follow
    electric saws cut steel—shrieks
    tea kettle whistle—pressure and friction:

    [agitated space]

blue skies disappear . . . deep purple
    unknown abyss forever?
    i stare and wonder

thick blades fresh green scented
    under my feet: earth
    solid i stand

and you, a few inches away
    your eyes, your gaze
    your essence images mine

        i experience other or another me.

cherries—lilacs—lavender
    intoxicate, impose
    intense pursuit, seize the source

reciprocal delight
    proximity/presence—distance/absence
    differentiate me and you

lose one—gain the other
    how far a burning fire, how close a bakery shop
    turn to signs, clues promise:

something exists, *what*?

hypnotic repetition
    water enchants
    stones splashed

delicious clear
    grazing country bells
    sleepy melodies

gestures no end message
    flow down luscious hills
    meander through valleys

    stream gushes between daffodils and buttercups

separate
    chunks of land
    mouth of the ocean draws

bobbing boats explore
    transport—commerce

sacred spaces of the ganges
    burning incense, red petals
    cleansing—rebirth
imperial ports
    phonecian—greek—roman
    scribes and scriptoria

open space
    egyptian seas, open land
    mosaic miracle chiseled into stone

freedom embraced
    migrants mix cultures:
        traders on horseback,
        merchants on sailboats

    south china sea below clouds wave

engulf power
    unfathomable volume
    o c e a n

im-penetrable
un-experienced
    minds of dizziness

quantify
    super-sensorial
    im-material space

        brains defied

dawn skies approach copenhagen,
        the nordic sun
           transforms pink clouds

red ball glows over the nile
        cairo from afar
        radiates prayerful calm

rio's copacabana reveals glorious sun
        rays pour over sugarloaf sand
        nature's exquisite breath

night-time darkness, lunar beams
        sky undressed
        tiny lights hide

changing positions, play tricks
        almost always there

fuller—emptier—brightness—blackness
        shines a path, horizon
        hides—hidden

                all disappear

captured by the self,
        liberated by being
        thinking creature absorbed


sublime beauty, natural order
        stars blanket black cosmos


soundless motion haunts
        stillness
        reaches out to the unreachable beyond


earth shares the galaxy
        martian—venereal—uranal—plutonic
        company

scattered beads on strings of light
        consistent predictable un-changing

              planetary force galactic balance maintains

uncertain when yesterday happened.
        how remote is the day before today?
        or how recent?

it occurred, it has passed, i am certain.

then, tomorrow, and its proximity.
        how can i speak of the un-happened?
        the un-real.

              even now does not exist.

substance separated
        knowable, non-perceptual
        intelligence engaged

divine cause
        angelic creature
        human soul

inductive methods
        discover occult mystery
        transcend corpo-reality

              union with ultimate being

knowledge beyond
        ... + ... + ... + ...
        affirming finitude

materiality unlimited
        =
        immateriality

undefined space
        substance non-sensorial
        mind as divine

sublime truth
    $2^2 + 3^2 = 4^2$
    always

eternal
    time and space
    conceptual-rational properties

does-not-rely-on-sense-data
    non-changing
    immutable
    non mutor

        principle
original source
    arche
    causes motion:
    mover alters space

        eternal Absolute

## Reminiscing in Blue

Neruda plays in my mind,
background
drama—notes I miss. Sipping coffee,
Saturday ritual in February sun,
day after a rainstorm.
Unholy words—destruction—
demolition disappear in the mist. Ocean recreates
my West Coast Island.
We watch the ferries
dock. My nephew hums with the boats.
Melody in past tense. Nostalgia.
Pacific Coast? Mamma and Papa?
Kids I brought to the beach?
Even then I missed them
with each *good-bye,* plane or ferry. How
many departures? I stopped counting.
Like the ocean waves they return.
Unending story to restore
what I lost. My innocence
in the nighttime sky
tasting the stars, smelling pure water
of a river, catching the music of spring blossoms,
melody of morning swallows tasted.

      As if I wait for someone?

## Heraclitus: Lessons at Dawn

The barren tree hangs—never
the same fuss.
Icicles drip—into the river—a current—
drops disappear in restless motion.
Tree stands crooked
as if still. Sun lasers—penetrable clouds
liquefying
crystalline layers—that stubborn trunk
trying not to move
—move the unhidden river—transparent,
subtle turbulence—
draws—
sucks—
even evergreen pines
resilience uncompromised—
silently succumb
to a non-same river.
Cones refuse to wave
to the river's victory.

## Saturday Morning

grey clouds
frame my window
                  ceaseless circles
                  coat below

uniform shades outside—and in

for my eternal headache
                        *red pills*

familiar sidewalks
crack before me

route repeats
my thought-less world

        bodies-in-motion struggle:

        drunkard—single car—empty bus

wet cement reflects flashing stop signs
unnoticed engineers
funds create
high-tech projects

coffee shop appears for sleepy patrons
                        insomniacs

        compulsive rituals

lost man staggers
        checks for coins
        in newspaper boxes

secured in a plastic bonnet a woman
        carts her bags down the street

some think friday night . . .
                              never ends
                              it did
music hides how i feel

who understands—
        enya's gaelic?

## Broken Glass
## or *Rethinking Kleist's "Das Zebrochne Krug"**

Shattered across a scent polished floor
pieces of crystal scattered
Czech treasure disappears
sweeping emotions, fragile history.

Heirlooms—traditions,
glass deconstructed,
reconstitute purpose in pieces,

or re-define the *thing*:

*smithereens* of decomposition
betray intelligence

tease affections to meditate
family-members—gift-givers:

      appears—dis-appears

          *is—is not*

      matter and form manipulated.

Deformed reality unknown,
in my mind the object hides

        *known* to me
        and still *is* . . .

*German playwright, Heinrich von Kleist, *Broken Jug* appeared in 1808.

# Shattered Child

Delicate fragile vulnerable
the world shocks the newborn
a hitting cry of life

      —secure love embrace
          baby yearns—

. . . walks, falls on a rough floor
whimpers become hot tears

        hugs & kisses?

                           Ice
cracks
    in rippling water
        vanishes

        in winter's fog and frost:

    child meditates eternity

    loaded thoughts
    naïve friend targets
        like shard glass
            to express affection

    —eyes betray
a ripped heart—

                mind probes,
                inquisitive
soul searches, hides.

Silent.

## Ember and Ash

Morning cigarette,
I suck the tobacco
sitting on steps. Smoke signals.
Rituals. David Hume fails to grasp,
sun rises, cigarette burns.
Rusty leaves curl
on piercing grass blades.
I wonder which will disappear first?

Country chapel stands, Church bell,
waits to knoll the next death.
Falling branches pencil black silhouettes.
I hear nothing, only a dog's bark.
Her panting breath, tongue hangs,
she surveys.
Non-sceptical St. Bernard keeps me
company.

I long for the short
winter days: nights at four,
silent darkness—
birds soar into non-existence,
maples dissolve into oblivion.
Fire meanders along the river,
waves of desire to be burned.

## Autumn Lake

Lake water
                      motions ripple?

Waves sedate me: numbness.

Dark granite-grey, abyss of spoken melancholy.

Sun pokes clouds

        pours orange and red
        on golden seagulls.

October soars in caws—fish & fear.

Park visitors paddle their canoe,

campfires extend their Summer.

Preys fenced—trapped.

Scent of autumn wishes
end already. Clouds unmoved settle

southwest

as if sunset keeps me from park
gates.

. . . last year someone disappeared.

## Last Night

He chops the wood axe-centred
Birch . . . Poplar . . . Oak: whack—split.
Fire devours the wood, midnight
ritual. Clouds drift, sky clears
to Verdi's *Seasons*.
Stars. Eternal Movers.
Sparrows chant like monks
at Vigils.
Church steeple hides the crescent moon,
veiled light undresses
the galaxy.
I dream of Aristotle writing
his *Ethics*.
My shirt is wrung in smoke,
embers rise at dusk,
without a morning hymn.

## You Sit on a Table

                    White linen
your eyes           bloodshot

sit upright—
barely.        Yes, late night
revelry
—over.

                Empty decanter,
brandy coats another.

Your          shoulder

bent forward
                in your colourful
                patch attire
                      Renaissance joker.

I like the Provençal chair
                legs under
                the tables
                sticking out
—to support her?

Sipping,            boots annoy

          green satin folds

cover the white blouse
                as if she waits . . .

He plays with your chestnut hair
with the black brocade on your
white flesh

candles flicker.

## Lost on the Tarmac

Airport announcements silence the tears
sad faces stand—wave
little and fragile.

Red-eyes at departure I bid
farewell
greet my dreams.

Five children—my dearest friends,

in cribs and beds each one asleep
I kiss
not knowing the details of their day.
One by one each fades
hidden
       on the road
       in the plane.

Attachments in Montreal
summers in Rome and Berlin
*au revoir* at the Paris tracks
truck departs the Zimbabwe mission
never returning to Cape Town.

Disappear.

Student societies—we studied together
marked by transforming our world.

Marriage temptations linger:

heart silent by engines.

# III

Cities and Fields

## In Brackets

He fell out of the window, shot dead.
I sat in the hotel lobby,
dinner appointment on the rooftop.
News reports a shooting two blocks away.
Drinking Pinot Grigio
with hazel nuts, I ignore the update.
*Killers fled.*
Vomit splattered in front of a Mexican restaurant
stinking urine beside an English pub,
colours of nausea fill me.
A man dead asleep on a warm air vent,
sleeping bags cover the grills.
Extended on her bench, a woman
lies hidden, unnoticed.
He occupies his corner, shivering
in his knitted winter hat
on cardboard
a college student begging.

CN Tower
rises above the city in clouds:
only guests
who earned the invitation
ascend.

## Danger: Overhead Work

Red splashes hammer words
                    hang on a green screen.
              Propane
cylinders secure in cages,
      cement slabs border
        stone structures—
tarred road.
He strides past in Blue Jays design;
she paces behind in tight jeans.
        *(of course, we ask, "why"?)*
        Orange and turquoise cab stops:
                pick up.
Diamond stones inserted
      in triangle rocks,
            carved into pyramids.
                Rosetta circle
                Industrial wheel,
     preparing to take off,
     blast into black star punctured
        sky:
                five engines
                trail of smoke.
Road cleared and empty,
massive black crater remains,
      and army shoppers,
        defending their bags.

## Blvd. de Maisonneuve

rap plays, I drink raspberry
hot chocolate
guy street and st catherine
concrete slabs rise
convents down, the block survives
as museums

rain drops caress, anticipate spring
wash away unwanted winter slush
pushy street traffic persists
bury struggling voices

victorian banks triumphant
echo the past,
relics —nostalgia of the grandeur empire,
avant-garde signals a new era
montréal, relentlessly post-modern

fusion: exotic thai—mexican salsa—
espresso—celtic pubs
the erotic—crisscrossed flags
seek the sacred, profane discovered
cosmopolitanism,
name of the new course

library books across tables strewn
usurp poverty, education's slogan
make endless love to laptops

forgotten street names pave new ones
only march refuses to change

## Western Tracks*

Italian Renaissance a triumphant cathedral
challenged by slabs of cement:

       Eternal lights reveal
       past protected.

Red and blue crosses
       at a crossroad.
       Buried blood stains
       forced monarchs, *United*.

Ancient capital announces, Kingston.

Fir tree—birch—maple—
       pine cones—thistles—branches—
streams . . . . . . rivers . . . . . . lakes . . . . . .

            under mourning clouds
       cabins and steeples join cemeteries.

Stretches of snow and ice meet in the sky
       village island identified
       black train track letters:
            *Allenwater Bridge,*

       smiles of the First Nations appear.

Tractors—trailers—pick-ups—
four wheel drives
           sea gulls hover and caw,
           Sioux Look-Out.

Orange . . . yellow . . . red mark another frontier,
bold sign posts and forests compete.

Flat fields stretch in silence
        wheat bushels . . .
                stacks of hay . . .
                        dusty road . . .

Red River welcomes immigrants on trains
kerchiefed women on Winnipeg posters.

Red grain elevator functions
not far from houses.
Men on tractors till open land—
cattle graze . . .
pink sun sets: Saskatchewan.

Land and water
        mixologist at work
                jet into clouds
                white transforms white
        rocks shelter elk—sheep—dear.

The Fraser River bows down to Moose Lake
Mt. Robson, Rocky's reference,
                      on duty.

        Waves meander,
        splash against black polished rocks.

Green treetops
pierce the skies,
        incline
                to the Pacific.

*4-day train—Montreal-Vancouver.

## Waking up between Continents

A collection of Caribbean birds
morning call,
aviary caws annoy me.
Pastel lines glow. Waves smash the rocks,
for the last five hundred years,
colonisers claim.
Flesh rhythms and fresh seaweed
boom and brush.
I drink the morning like
mango juice.
Mother runs out, spins a frisbee,
Afro in Anglo-Dutch tones, roasts
Chorizo to Spanish drums.
Humid odour of damp walls
and hotel towel
re-trace images of East Africa.
But these islands? Another story.
Flags of rival monarchs
history bubbles in.
Royal blood, Regaton syllables.
Isabella's religion remains,
her baptizing patron cleared the way.
Latin vowels still roll.

*San Juan de Puerto, Rico.*

# Arkansas Weekend

Church steeples and Crosses,
stretch on endless roads
I stop at the liquor store:
*Southern Comfort,*
my county is dry.
The wisteria vines and flowers paint in mauve,
pines like officers spray green needles
along the route.
Discover real pull-pork
and brown or white gravy. I request the brown,
the waitress, calls me darl'n,
explains the white. Pretty southerner
soothes me
with her accent, smile and wink. I try
fried green beans, catfish on a Friday,
and hushpuppies. Order Fat Tire
in El Dorado.
Spanish and French flags displayed.
Sitting by the river
I read poetry and listen
to her Southern fiction.
We lament:
created illusion.

## Rhoda's Tamales

Leaving Drew county,
where Monticello
displays a Queen Anne home, majestic
invitation to society's upper echelons—
once upon a time—Neoclassical
and Gothic? Façades relate
a narrative, I withdraw.
County roads eclipse highways
merge into silence of cattle grazing,
fertilized fields of soya, high level
water for rice and into Chicot county,
cotton plantations.
Narrow corridor, tarred and dirt,
shaded by oak and pine direct
to the village, where cotton grows,
and plantations spread.
I stopped at the little restaurant,
white house offering *food for the soul*.
Rhoda greets me
sitting
where she greets her customers
worked for years and her smile
forms a southern drawl.
Beside me, US flags and a map of Arkansas,
I remove the husk, eat the inside
of six tamales spiced
with Louisiana hot sauce.
I smile at the warm pecan pie
and fluffy sweet potato pastry.
Sitting at her table gracious
as if in prayer, Rhoda smiles.

## Altar of MonteAlbán*

Lush green screams in red soil,
solid granite rises like a flattened pyramid,
architect or astronomer's configuration.

Trembling hands raised to the sky—
terrifying gods, dressed in anger,
smell the offering.

Prepared virgins or captured soldiers
resist their destiny.

Stripped to satisfy swords of divinities,
sorcerer chants, hands raised to heaven,
exhorts the gods in his trance.

Wood burns, fire glows—a snake hissing.
Smoke delights inhaling nostrils.

Black night is pierced by sacred stars
temples aligned,
altar configured.

They disappear—
the sorcerer rattles bones.

*Monte Albán, Oaxáca, Mexico

## Septima

In regal corridors
processional columns,
> I meditate
>> statues of saints.
>> Clouds hover.

Staring into *Septima* I dream
sipping coffee
> Colombian
> alone
> deafened
>> by traffic
>> telephone calls
>> sellers
>> candy merchants.

With others I find shelter
> at an experienced bank—
> July rains pour
> on helpless by-standers
> whistle for taxis,
> or stand under VIP umbrellas.

A young boy wears his pea-coloured jersey
and black pants
> picks up hail stones
> melt in his hands.
>> Startled
>> by the thunder
>> he hesitates
>> his back-pack firmly attached.

                    Dashes out.

Rich children in uniforms expect
chauffeurs to pick them up
—waiting—playing soccer.

Exhaust fumes along Septima—
greasy *chorizo*\* sizzles—*erepas*\* all day      \*sausage/\*griddle corncake
Seconds to cross a pot-hole road
merciless cars.

Yellow cabs claim the lanes,
annoy the beggars on each block
too tired to beg, covered in plastic bags
sleeping in midafternoon.

Dreamy students spot the bars
                    rush
                    out of class
                    to salsa.

Sacred hands wave
            I approach dizzy.
Baroque Churches, Spanish mystics,
—Bogota on *Septima*.

## Soaking Rwanda

        Hairline—height
        income—education.

Rampage begins:

    arms and ammunition
    centres-of-command
    to-execute.

    Wild youth, Interahamwe—
    white—red—green extremists

    machete marches

    peasant axes.

Army prepares its surgical mission:
single target—
        national killing machine
        slaughter for security.

    Propaganda controls thought.

Friends turn-into spies—sell-outs—murderers,

Blood despised: blood shed.

Nine hundred thousand too late.

    Stench-of-blood villages.
    Red-drenched mud roads.

    River damned by corpses.

        World watched Rwanda soak.

## Tribute to Mandela

I visited Soweto in eighty-six—
organised tour—
celebrated my birthday
alone
at a Pizza Hut in Johannesburg.

      You: a prisoner in jail.

Suid Afrika, what do you think?

I used the only trains from Harare
or *Salisbury*—my students teased:
Net Blanke—SAR.*                        *South African Railways

      Sanctions failed to remove
      *Whites Only* in the 80s!

Blacks share their buses
with *me*.

Lost at Ladysmith I hop
into a combi
asked a Zulu squeezed beside me

      for his help

          in Bloemfontein
          we disembark
          he leads me
          to my Orange Free State lodging.

Elections in ninety-four,
British Airways and Portuguese Airlines
announce: ready to evacuate nationals.

In Cape Town university students sit
secure: opposite sides
at classroom tables—in front of me:

Blacks                          Whites

*University of Cape Town*
*April, 1994*

## Atlantic Desert, Southwest*

Kilometres of tarred road
melt—sun torches. Sky announces

>*end approaches*

>>orange and purple
>>velvet curtain.

Black-like lava pours—

wind haunts in high-pitched syllables.

>Lunar sand dunes
>>rise like silos—

>create massive walls
>barricade me—in my sealed world

>>my body numb.

Namib fossils lie wordless
>>soul-less.

Gaze at me hopeful
I can relate their story. My journey

>accompanied by prehistoric
>stones.

White waves foam
Atlantic abruptly crashes
>gulls impose their screech.

Along Namibian shores
                    pink pelicans dance.

*\*Kaprivi Strip/Swakomund*

## Across the Sinai

I bid my Egyptian friends . . . farewell,
    congested bus I board in Cairo

        fourteen-hour journey . . .
                across the Sinai.

Indefinite goodbye injects pain
dread of a desert tourist.

Turquoise postcards
    of pharaohs offer child-like
        distraction . . .

Mangos my lunch—juice drips—sticky
    fingers
    fold skin into a newspaper-napkin.

Dusty peninsula before me, I wander
aimlessly . . .

I am driven to my destination:

    I trust the road
    stretch through date palms,

    no signs of a Calf.

Crusty lips chapped in a line, passport control.

    My mouth dry, I dream:
    flight
    university . . .

    in the desert.

## Gulf Windows

        Mountains stretch
rip into Turkey and Iran,
          jagged blue rivers
                tiny distant villages.
                        I land
on an airstrip of images.
        Our plane leaves Tehran,
        route to Mumbai,
        Karachi awaits us.
                Persian Gulf/Arabian
not far from Dubai, pilot announces.

My . . .
        drive to Aqaba . . . , 3$^{rd}$ class to Luxor,
dreams of Beirut—Damascus—Bagdad,
                crushed.
        Adolescent hopes
                —flattened.
River branches red.
        I transfer to Goa
where Portuguese left fishing nets.

# Relics of Goa

Ships vanish, Indian waves
spray white crests,
sunlight, sand hides spiders
sea gulls soar, caw.
Tale of colonisers who disembark,
boats sail the coastal seas,
*a casa*\**house
*a igreja*\**church
*a cidade*\**city
disappear in the horizon of history.
Sunk. Drowned. Diseased.
Ocean shouts loudest
in palm tree chorus
shores in centuries of silence,
crab undisturbed
crawls
out of its hole, brushing across the seaweed.

## Bombay Lights

Bollywood colours the clouds,
Mumbai welcomes me in electric images
on a Saturday midnight.
Coastal landing, Indian ocean lights,
A340 graciously descends.
Narrow streets, uneven buildings,
sheets of water reflected.
Floral carpets, smell of dampness,
panelling lined with Indian stars
trigger
the teak of my first New Delhi Hotel
and Sikh taxi driver.
Thoughts re-focus on chai masala, sweet,
vegetarian samosas.
Rain pellets spray the airport,
roof and windows washed.
Airport security, Indian military in Khakis,
usual body check procedures.
Conveyor belts continue,
metal detectors, airport bus boards,
4:30am.
Domestic terminal now obsolete,
new terminal flashes shiny floors,
floral lighting dim,
moveable sidewalks, extended space.
Food fair offers world famous chicken
and the global coffee logo,
late-night shopping, bar lounges,
passengers asleep.
Plastic signs of cities

replaced with computerised info.
Airline agent still appears,
first morning call:
*Chennai—Chennai*. I wait for *Goa*
without *chai*,
*they ran out of tea masala.*
At least Rabir Kapoor
rescued me in a wall-size add,
when I heard, *Namasate*.

## Bollywood Moves

Eros of Indian drama, thematic—
predictabile: unions authorised
or forbidden—
arranged/love marriage.
Leila's caste hates Raj's clan.
Political moves, army/crime:
tension: resolution:
adrenalin dance, bolly moves.
Camera focusses on a goddess,
red-orange-yellow sari,
henna art, body jewels.
Rejected lover in his ripped jeans,
unbuttoned shirt,
roughed up relentless
fighter fist clenched demands
justice or revenge:
*one-two-three-get on the dance floor*:
charged bodies connect.
Rite of religion.
Honour unlimited.
Masala spices, flesh energy
synchronised: cinnamon, coriander
cardamom.
The End: hot mango pickle.

# Tea Ceremony

I attempt the Tea Ceremony
move my bowl away from my lips
to rest—violating sips.
Her father drinks all the tea
as if a shot glass. I feel foolish.
A need to apologise?
Noriko smiles,
her mother and father, too.

A simple ceremony, I broke
the rule.

Perhaps I should have prayed
at the Shinto shrine
where rice and oranges remain
in silence before black and white
photos of her ancestors.

She graciously leads me
to the tea house
like her play puppy.

The maple branches,
someone's jewellery box
—Japanese garden.

Winding the key a curious boy listens:
my first piece of Beethoven.
Not music or jewellery or house
but the green-trimmed space. Ferns, bonsai,
a wooden bridge over a river,
in hills an isolated country house
. . . on the red box.

I inhale the wood, taste the stream.
Dreaming from my house in cotton
pyjamas,
I drink the winding key.

*Nagoya, 1988*

# IVa

OrangePortraits

## Scent of Copenhagen

   Tarmac ride begins—taxi

  separated

by a link fence, sixties buildings
   injected with new taxes
     marked airliner,

—shakes—motionless.

Summer traffic, smog and humidity
smell.

    [Family faces name my fate.]

Thrilled by noise, a novice driver:
airport—my garage—my warehouse

bodies and engines
wings widen and narrow:

     I signal them on the ground
     from my massive window.

Midnight melodrama
mechanical visits, I sip night-time coffee:

   nothing changes except
     gate extensions: refitted planes
     departures/arrivals
     exotic languages.

... mamma approaches, red eyes—

       my first flight at sixteen: Copenhagen—
       family waits in southern Italy.

papa : sister & fiancé :—confused:
                             *are you sure?*

Airports my dream—my agony.

## La Haïtienne

Focussed in a Spanish class
my professor from Bar-ce-[*the*]-lona,
        fricates her inter-dentals.

Student behind me puts her hand
on my head ties my hair, her comments
in Quebecois
                      entertain me.

But with a Haitian classmate—*friend*—
we switch from English to French
              . . . attempt our Spanish.

Her apartment, Sherbrooke street res,
we share lunches at the student caf.

La Haïtienne brings me a bottle,
her mom's creamy Port au Prince liqueur.

Twenty years later, we re-unite in Montreal,
greetings with a kiss, Italian dinner.

Married with three children, her career
and politics—her story of success.
        I wondered about her *happiness* . . .

        Intense, her eyes:

        Accident on slippery roads,

hit    by    two    cars,
reassured, protected by Mary
              and her medal.

In a filing cabinet folder I empty my room,
I find my friend's
                melancholy poem . . .

That favourite Haitian bottle,
I still taste
the creamy sweetness.

            My gift to her, a Rosary.

# Donut Shop

Bushy hair—worn face—
he claims his coffee. Yellow-stained fingers
rip an apple fritter from his teeth.

Itinerant narrates a desperate
story—lost his change—needs
early morning company.

Mundane routine—re-visited.
Useless occasion to gather
on sleepless nights—all five possess
a table—shouting in pharyngeal syllables.

Late hour fatigue for the taxi driver,
driven by carbo cravings—caffeine
fix—and cheap customers.

Ceiling lights flash *open for business*—
black coffee pours
crullers and raspberry-filled doughnuts
on display.

Client attempts to pay waving
his dirty coupon.

## Carpenter in the Winter

The vagabond scrapes ketchup
off the Morning Sun: he throws it on the floor
checking for more scraps. His plastic knife
works like a chisel.
Exhaling white circles, coffee breath,
the loose scarf creates a passage to his
salty beard. Mucus frozen
drips like snotty icicles.
Knitted hat pulled to the side,
covers half his ears.
Curved back hidden between parked cars.
Eyes fixed on plastic take-outs,
slice of salami, couple of fries,
even onions.
Black Winter furs, red poinsettias,
French after shave, unnoticed.
Carving like a carpenter,
until he reaches
the next garbage can.

# Sherbrooke Street

**VIII.** Victorian brick houses framed,
        rose gardens line the streets.
            Maple trees and birch direct a procession

point to the equinox

summer rain smashes into the canopy.

                          **IX.** Chatter
occupies the lawns, returning students.

Smell of cotton—acrylic—
                    leather bags
                    plastic binders—

      bulging back packs
      suede boots

                fill the open space.

*Com, psych, bi, poli sci* compete in timetable talk.

Late afternoon cheers echo across fields.

Statue of Angels untouched.

            **X.** Dew on morning grass,
leaves scatter:

            silk green smudged into soft
            yellow
            red.

Campus grounds on canvas paper.

**XI.** Dreary clouds hang

motionless

soggy green layers—leaves fade,
yellow clings.
Black trunks, detailed branches in clouds.
Music indoors
surrounded by the future
. . . darkness looms at 3pm.

Old cinema remains—*out of place*—Egyptian art—pharaohs opposite a golden-leaved park.

**XII.** Snow spreads her cotton wings
into winter space:

students in exam mode ignore
lullaby melodies
        wood carvings
           red=blue=green lights.

Can a scent from twenty years ago linger? Student explores independence, unwritten projects.

Empty small apartment offers shelter
from icy winds.

Cosmopolitan faces unchanged
        trendier styles scream
        exotic languages my children would speak,
        in dreams.

**I.** Campus corridors . . . that language lab where we first met. Snow-covered January steps,
night-time chill.

Extended conversation after French . . .

        with her.
        . . . I thought she might be there.

**II.** Mom descends on the escalator,
Canadian mink at Dorval:
    -lasagna for her son
    -Ziploc minestrone for months
    -business contacts
    -Toronto next—Milan, then back West
    -seven days.

                      **III.** Month in-
between,
    slushy snow
    remains
    freezes hardens
    pellets

imposed on Spring.

**IV.** Good Friday rains cover the campus.
Gray fills the chapel, clouds clamour
reconcile me with God
                      and her.

She stands outside holding an umbrella.

**V.** Summer studies, sidewalks cleaned,
unwanted snow surrenders:
              cheery sun, sticky rain,
              bluejays eavesdrop.

                        **VI.** Late
library nights—slides repeat:
        I study in the same sweat:
        notes
        philosophy
        texts.
I wonder, *Where is she?*

**VII.** Maple leaves affirm after one year
—after twenty:

velvet caresses, branches wave.

Heavy humidity felt,
        cafeteria music—beats unchanged.
        I follow the route to my apartment
        in the dark.

... I studied Descartes, humid month
with the Rationalists once again
        in summer melodies—

                      I hold
the syllables of our class hands out.
*English Lit*, she teaches, pretends not to notice me—
returns to her text—deliberately.

                      Alone—
French love songs tease me on the radio,

                thoughts of her ...

A cyclist rolls into the parking lot
someone I recognise:

        lessons on Aristotle's, *Ethics*.

Neo-gothic chapel hides history,
virgin statue intercedes—Stoic harmony:
        arms stretch that flowering grotto
        where water flows.

Child plays in the grass—perhaps my own.

Life I constructed at a crossroads:
        dark blue sky holds a thin moon.
        Past the familiar corner I stroll
        where I bid her farewell

                on a street ...

## Pigeon Lady

A mannequin's posture, the lady reflects
sunrise—creates an intense glow.

Snagged nylons at the knees she advertises
her floral print coat, looping layers
of turquoise dress.

Her arms outstretched, open palms
display assorted seed—main attraction.

Standing as if molded in her location,
lady's head follows her companions
circle—tickle—pecking presence.

Shoppers race past, business people
pace wired to cells, seekers of bargains
and contracts.

Pigeon Lady unnoticed except
her aviary company constant.

Streetlights flash—cars brake
days uninterrupted . . .

Pigeon Lady disappeared:
nobody noticed except thrusting pigeons.

At home the weakened woman lied
in her damp bed, sweating in a fever,
too sick to feed her feathered friends.

Her apartment empty, cracked walls
curtains tattered, for years pipes leaked.

Beaks tap at her window sill.

## Leather-Tapper

Entertained on rue Saint Catherine,
country dance rhythms repeat:

two wooden instruments
tap—tap—tap, tap-the-leather.

Focussed, he sits in khaki shorts
forgets his beggar's wage

street corner labour when shop opens
for lunies and tunies and paper notes.

Sidewalk partitioned for his stage,
owns the spot where he performs:

Elbow-on-knee tap-the-leather,
Ogilvy signals his block.

Wears his leather hat in autumn,
body motions to square dance.

Snow-ploughed streets, warmed
in winter gloves, beats for Christmas.

Music makes a merry season
endless jingles singing box.

Behind belts and wallets, his eyes
hidden, story unknown

. . . on my last walk, thirteen years
later, the tapper disappeared. And I

never asked for a piece of music.

# Aufwiedersehen

    June flights to study *deutsch*,

morning yawns—drowsy afternoons.

Pens put aside—books closed:
    at the *Garten,* Warsteiner
    regurgitates Goethe's language!

Strolls down Bremen's *Strassen,*
pronounced guttural frication
    I was taught to repeat, *leise.* *      *softly

    Deutsch I exercised
at the *Hauptbahnhof,* *      *central train station
I listen—wait . . .

My latinised consonants interfere,
    sonoric vowels inserted . . .

    \*\*\*\*\*

Friend from Paris, we opt for French:

    Dutch tulips decorate
    Marktpltaz and the nordic Roland.

Hand in hand
I sang with morning doves:

    German syllables
    heard at splashing fountains.

*Deutsche Bahn,*\*                                    \**German Railroad*
journey east through closed borders,
even Dobermans sniffed the wagons.

We tasted poems until Berlin . . .

        blitzing city lights
        Volkswagen
        black leather and Saxon blonds.

At a Moroccan restaurant
we exchanged hopeful dreams . . .

I embrace her from afar, she stands
waves good-bye at the Gare de Lyon,

        and fades with the motion
        of train . . . tracks . . .

Notre Dame t-tshirt to remember.

        We never prayed about eternity,
        and forgot the stress on,

        *auf wieder sehen.*

## Father's Day at My Desk

    Boxes bounce off his little hand,
    sun-splashed trees drips orange juice.

Red licorice strings—
kisses for papa.

               Arms stretch
she dances in her pony-tail,
       freckles laugh
         into his cotton arms.

Papa carried me on Friday nights
              as I dreamed
along cool streets hidden under trees.

He spat at the cinema
cheering black and white Hercules.

Lunch—*pranzo*\*—southern Italy        \*main meal/lunchtime
silver poured on white table cloths.

African War repeated clips:
. . . I carved his journey from Ethiopia
to South Africa.

Mail and phone calls trickle
             to absent.

Books and semesters promise a future
computer keys—now digital company—
electronic messages, screen.

             Papa's formatted stories

echo in my room:              unfinished.

After the movies I bought Macintosh toffee.
            I made a white paper house
            at night where the toffee

                        sleeps.

## Mr. Penny

He fills his sock with about five thousand or more, stopped by airport security—X-ray—search, and boards his flight. Godmother's
knit scarf, hides in thick blue. Tibetan hat with braids, priest's gift. He likes to pay in copper coins counted in advance.
*Not much good* one clerk glares, *a hassle,* another smirks, *we don't really take pennies.* He fills out *satisfaction* forms, pleased with two dollar discounts.
Complaints ensure free combos—shows off manager's reply.

Sometimes he feels like Dr. Jeckyll when he stands
before his students and lectures on ethics.

# Whatever Happened to Baby . . . ?

Tower hides southwest. Sunset
withdraws behind the river:
iron bridge covers secret shadows
bushes embrace darkness.
Yellow streetlights process
to the neo-Gothic Church,
cars slide on whitened streets.
Between my tower and the arch
Chinese take-out and Vietnamese pho.
Easter chocolates I eat at Christmas,
Texas fruitcake,
my dinner—with St. Remy.
Gifts.
Packaged food for locked occasions.
I am not seen roaming corridors.
Escape
through bolted gates.
Final run:

I don't need a car to drive over me.

## Table for One—Two Years Later

Ice pellets shut me in the corner
pastry shop.
Deep snow paralyses December shoppers
off Laurier avenue. Risky drivers skid.
My psychiatrist
tells me I cannot return
to that corner
where I bid her farewell.
      Every year
      a love story
      reconstructs fantasy.
My ritual I continue at *Gascogne*
with tea—teaspoon in my mind.
*Mr. Hotdog,* campus fast food, landmark
before and after classes. He witnessed our
separation—her last words.

I hold them like her hands.

# Again

her presence
filled my nostrils.
There, in the leaves. *Why do you hide?*
Refuse to ignore caresses once dreamed.

Her

cyprinum fragrance, evening mist
occurrence of illusion

evaporates at the crossroads
Where syllables transform destiny:

final *I Do*.
choked *No*.

How different the pages written in solitude
far from home; if not a twenty-one year old.

Innocent daytime strolls, surrounding maples
icy skies after evening classes . . .

acceptance . . .

refusal stacked like files . . .

*Why do you still whisper?*

[What if?]

# Vb

## CLINIC Doors/Recovery

# Appointment

Calm voice—soothing father
displays the photo.
                I examine the scene
as the psychiatrist instructs:

      little boy
      six . . . perhaps
      wearing shorts
      white t-shirt

      stands
      in front of a remote cabin
      alone,

*What do you see?*

*I see a happy boy*
*free*

the boy's journey begins
unaccompanied

          eyes search
          sensitive

unhindered movement . . .

years pass
          wood chopped
          fires lit

          healing cuts.

## Emergency

Red symbols flash, my flesh tickles—
                I am folded on a bench
        cries of children
        woman screams
                flee past me.

Shrieks terrify me.

Black and white photos of women
standing together. Nuns.

Coated in tears, veiled in mourning
scarves like a Flemish crucifixion.

Prairie fields and mountains separate
me.
        Abyss of unknown.
        Alone.

Worn out slush-covered boots,
        knitted wool scarf,
            heavy blue coat and tuque.

        I feel . . .
        my heartbeat . . .

Blood pressure—ECG—nurse examines me,
probing fingers, sensitive hazel eyes.

        Strange love pulsates within.

Name tag recalls my maternal source
—and father.

    Stretched, I lie in my blue

            cotton gown.

## Admitted*

I enter the dark room, grey reminds
me, he doesn't have visitors. Stretched in his bed,
he waits, and acts as if he still has his
left leg. I am not used to the scars myself:
incisions—cut—amputation.
I visit him often, but I don't have
answers. Perhaps, my comments offend?
He may not wish to see me, but I will return.
A dedicated nurse intervenes
asks for support.
I continue with the other patient,
to listen
—his childhood stories dominate his thoughts:
nostalgia, wonders whether he will
return home to his family,
or his apartment . . .
tears of the unknown,
disturb—frighten: incertitude.
Curtains drawn, odour emerges
from the adjacent bed. I want to visit him.
I waited. He seemed too young
for a stroke, his right arm unmovable,
his fixed discourse rich in ideas, but
difficult to articulate. And his comprehension,
as if I spoke a foreign language.
I jot words and phrases to communicate,
words he reads—as if in darkness. I repeat
syllable-by-syllable.
She refers to me as "drop dead gorgeous,"
I am not sure why

I feel uneasy.
She wishes to connect with me
and does not
remember who I am.
Her conversations and her humour
engage, then, she questions me,
I'm never sure . . . how to answer. I promised I'll be back.
I spoke to his wife, but he disappeared,
and, where did she go?
Only to find the two of them in the corridor.
She pushed him in his wheelchair, *eh Joe,*
instead of *Giuseppe.*
His smile conveyed
security of his wife's presence, who still prepared
his *minestra.*\* She shaved his beard, combed         \*soup
his hair, and brought him for a stroll.

       \*\*\*\*\*\*\*

Dance music fills the aisles. I look for onions,
then, tomatoes, the crushed ones I do not find,
and so, I compromise with diced.
Lovers kiss beside me.
I continue to the sugar section, hoping to find
raw sugar. A woman speeds
down the aisle. I wonder what her
problem is. Everyone races
to the checkout counters. I shop for my
Saturday dinner, cheese platter with walnut
and dried cranberry. Liquor store for Port,
clerk recommends Taylor Fladgate,
—perhaps for Sunday after lunch.
Irritation on my left side—extends to my arm,
and my toes . . .
Why does everyone rush?

   A version of "Admitted" was read at the *Blue-Met Literary Festival*
   (Montreal, April 28-29, 2017).

## December's Paradox

Short days of winter freeze a family; thick gray clouds fix overhead like an omen determined to deliver and fulfill its message: the news of a dead husband-father-brother-uncle who finds life too agonizing to live, and bids the world farewell, his way, OD'd, requesting ashes to be blown across the living soil that gave him life.

December fills the air with colours of familiar paradox: lights decorate barren branches dispel myths of sunless days claiming victory over eternal black. Communal corridors transmit unwanted colds and coughs and flus. Diarrhea dehydrates. Another harmless seasonal bug sends a frail nun to the hospital; ripped from her prayers, the woman lies flat on a hospital bed; her face disappears —her fragile body is no more. Few know her story. The newspapers and television, the radio and the internet, forgot to tell it.

Not so old, that gentle heart left the world with her soul. Snow falls outside hospital windows, but the moans of an aching youth forgets childhood thoughts. Odours overpower of clinical panels, scent of fake pines. Patients moan in a room for one securing four. Weeks pass, the young man wonders why the doctors won't let him go. Tests —more tests —bacterial infection —pneumonia —CT-scan —who knows? His birthday disappears, too.

Another coffin hides the season's wreaths and ribbons. He knew he was given six months or less after a visit to the specialist for stomach pains and vomiting; time to prepare his farewells, from house to hospital to palliative care to funeral home and cemetery. Goodbyes he repeats in painful motion, not knowing his last.

Sudden death, they said, the robust woman just fainted and died. She casually marched to the table to take an apple. And fell. The paramedics were powerless. Grey clouds, loud and mean, refuse to leave. Heaps of solid snow barricade streets, nature has its own way of burying.

The deceptive sun shines ruthlessly across magnetic blue skies; turquoise-green waters laced with blades of white foam —unsuspecting forceful nature hides merciless vengeance. Luscious velvet leaves seduce with tropical fruit, pineapple, mango, papaya, guava tease and tickle the innocent. Children laugh their freedom uninhibited —unrestrained. Grown-ups play stress-reducing adult games. Nature takes over: natural cotton fibers stretch across kilometers of sandy beaches, palm leaves wave, like half-mast flags wind viciously howls. Yellow, orange green scatters between sky—ocean. Wild animals possess secret information they share. Supernatural energy of a natural order defies intelligent creatures; their confidence in useless technology.

Vulnerable disappear. And the dead must be buried. December: that month of artificial lights and heavy darkness, holiday laughter and joy-filled promises, when nature controls, transforms the world into mourning —and a morgue.

## Hiding MySelf

    In a circle, chairs we occupy
                group of seven,
moderator observes
        —interpretation.
                      I am invited
to speak—*express*—become *vulnerable*,
like extroverts—or be *evicted*
        my fears!
        icy glances!
        Shirley Jackson's *Lottery,* rips.
            I fear conflict:
            they know my "Swamps."
I am a snail secure in its shell,
                . . . rays
of light        call me out.
I stand as a human encased in feeling:
                Voice tense, pitch low
unsettled by their words,
my words are charged
        with *me,*
    my heart runs in syllables, I am on
a track field, baton in my hand.

    I am hit—trip—flat,
    nose bleed:
    my contained thoughts
            honest words—*be honest . . .*

On my feet, just when my baton reaches out—
mistaken rescue: bang!
                                Karpman's triangle.
Rescuer, now prosecuted,
               catch me
               like a treat
               I become victim.

I am the snail
        I return to my shell
        though I felt rays
        of sun calling me out . . . .

## It's Getting Dark

Her bruised face—I'm not always sure
of the condition.
I smiled and introduced myself.
She told me her name. Then,
she stared at the ceiling. I observe
the catheter. She looks at her fingers,
she tells me about her needle-weaving.
Then, her thirst.
She drinks water. Her eyes focus on me,
*You're a patient man.*
I smile, reply. She turns her head,
perhaps, she did not hear,
or was it her medication, maybe
condition? Her eyes re-focus on the corridor,
*will they be long?* I wondered whom,
and ask. She replies with silence,
and tells me, *it's lonely here.*
And I inform her,
*I am here with you.*
She stares at me,
*you're a good friend.* I sit in my chair,
with a yellow gown and latex gloves.
She stares at the clock
over my head. *They always take so long.*
I smile and wave goodbye, and from the door
I watch her hands wave in the air.

## Sounds in My Head

Beeps.
        Blood rush.
                Colour codes.
        Saturday afternoon
Thursday evening
              shifts.
Who knows.
        I work on charts,
        just before I sign—out
eight-thirty pm.
        Announcement:
             familiar
              colour, code alert!
CODE BLUE-CODE BLUE-CODE BLUE
I approach the unit
medical team at work.
        I meet the family.
             We wait:
                    We watch:
              We wait:
              We watch:
Prayers . . .
Silence . . .
I hear a familiar beep,
flat sound—won't go away.
Green line . . . diagonal . . . flat . . .
I listen . . . on the subway:
            Beep . . .
            Tears . . .
            Cries . . .

Body blessed . . .
Prayers . . .
                Beep . . .
                Beep . . .
At midnight I arrive home.
Beeeeeeeep . . . . . . . . . . . . . . . . . .

## Isolated

        I                hear
my      name
                pro-lo-nged

excitement,
                                Voice
I recognise—
as if a forgotten friend
                       Eyes in her

                     direction

then mine.         She accompanies . . .
              me
                   to her room,
past
the station.
without an emergency alert—in case.
                       My *friend*
                             brings
                             me
                             to her room
which puts a desert monk to shame:
-bed
-lights
-blackboard
-window.
                   Her voice hoarse,
                   she tells me to wait.

Door opens,
                        she leaves
                        with permission;
as I sit
on             her           bed,
walls white                 writing
                                    on the board
erased
                        another cloudy day.

                        Mattress
uncomfortable.

I have nothing to distract me
or keep me busy.
I wonder how long           before she
              r e t u r n s.
My hair falls over my eyes as eye look
down.
My hands folded on my knees,
                        I occupy
                        the room
                        —alone
                        ——observed
                        ——isolated.

## Delirium or Delusion

Sun pours purple rays of delirium
the void I know. Metallic blue sky
of winter death suffocates—I
don't know why. Theatre images
surface, cannot be changed, soaked
in the past . . . drown me. Frozen
river I cross—a bridge—
children laugh ice skating
outside my head.
I am walled by iron and stone,
in a meandering direction,
a green surface I cannot reach.
My devoured heart still beats.
I only wish I had taken
that first exit.

   . . . because the voices will not stop!

## Tram I Won't Forget

    He laid in his bed,
    eyes slightly open,
    unkempt hair
    staring up—
    as if still on the stretcher.
Voice almost inaudible, he related
his story:
        His tram.
        Stop request.
      Disembarking passenger.
         Car failed to stop.
         Accident with no injury.
I listened. A stranger,
I would again be unknown—
I returned:
        He lied down.
        He sat up.
        He walked.
Until one day I heard he was discharged,
probably without knowing that,
    I cared—felt what he felt.
    When a tram approaches, I feel:
driver
stop
passenger
car . . . hospital . . .

# Morning from the Hospital

Smell of disinfectant—hospital bed linen—
lab coats—surgical dress

fragile patients
                  surround me

                          . . . thoughts of mamma.

                  Vancouver clinic
repeated late-summer visits,

over twelve months have past.

Massive concrete, steel slab
structures stand—ignore me.

High-rises diminish Montreal churches
silenced by endless construction
clamour.

Sun tickles—
overwhelms me. Crying creatures
emerald park invitation:

        hang onto branches
        play with sunlight.

Azure sky stretches bearded in white.

Brown squirrel dances

to distract me.

## Junction

Rough patch of road, green fields
whisper your name.
Gray clouds shape into anger
armoured for punishment.
Your face at every junction
coaxes and crushes
my red ears, my mangled body,
the many *you's*.
On this stretch between the bells
of paradise and the ashes of hell
you refuse to go away.
How small the plots of wheat
compared to an eternal moment:
*you*. My heart is chiseled by your
jealous love, hands kneading me
into existence.
Your fragrance seduces me
—into *being*.

## Silent Syllables

Your silent soul journeys
at dawn,
traces of morning mist,
purple and pink,
you take my hand, yours, I feel the cold.
The eternal lamp, you shine
on my soul.
You fill my empty cups
with your immortality
and delicately knead my
sorrows with your fragrant drops.
Frozen ponds, and cracked ice,
ruminate your quiet kisses.
And yet,
How can I contain your timeless thoughts?
You offer in ancient urns,
your yes. But mine is maybe.
Bushy pines and layered firs,
whip the wind,
Only syllables I hear, a language
unknown.
Words written with feathers.
I stare into the whiteness of life,
looking for its distant end, invisible,
just so I can hope,
and wonder about you.

# Ecstasy*

Her feet stick out, clinical blue sheets
cover her body. Wicker mat hair unveils
arctic eyes, rotting yellow teeth.
Her smile broken, icy nails pierce my palm.
Empty window to the left signals winter:
black stiff crows, grey ocean waves, caw and pour
into our room. My hand released from a clammy grip,
three syllables uttered: *Am I God?*
She smudges in colours—*Sagittarius.*
I examine the cloudless sky:
stars and belt, whisper, *Chiron.*[1] Room contains
horse hair, bearded face. Pointing to his body, pumping heart,
arrow directs to the moon. He shoots.
Wings flap, I am fastened on a saddle,
white horse, *Pegasus* in flight.
Starry path leads east, feathers like a shield glide
on clouds. Sun chants over the Ganges. We descend
into rocky hills, *there,* a cave. I read the forgotten manuscript.
Earth-coloured skirt wraps around my waste, Indian
knot his grandfather taught me. Granite walls, cool breeze
separate us. My hands fold at my heart, *namaste,*[2]
I offer my guru. Scrolls—*Upanishads*[3]:
first stage—*detachment.*
I step off the boat, sun over the Nile,
palm trees of Thebes, desert, beyond. I whip
the camel south—Valley of the Kings.

1. *Chirion,* half man-half horse in Greek mythology.
2. *Namaste,* Hindi, "greeting the divine presence in the other."
3. *Upanishads,* Hindu religious manuscripts (800–300 BC).

Nefertiti,[4] she bows to the One among Many.
In her eternal sleep, the tomb marked,
I sweat in the enclosed chamber, protected—
bewitched, I lick my lips.
From the Acropolis Plato observes the stars at night;
I am immobilized by Athena's temple columns.
We contemplate planetary alignment:
Diotima's heavenly Ideas thrown,
catch Immortal Beauty.[5]
Shutters rattle in sacred Umbrian hills.
On her knees the ground vanishes, numbness absorbed.
The woman of Foligno,[6] her arms outstretched,
angel wings, light, while she bleeds. Shaking,
hot candles burn. Melting blood drips.
We stare through the ceiling.
In secret syllables I taste Eternity.

*A version of "Ecstasy" was read at the *Blue-Met Literary Festival* (Montreal, April 28-29, 2017).

---

4. *Nefertiti* (ca. 1370-1330 BC, co-regent, wife of the pharaoh, "Akhenaten," and with equal power).

5. Plato' *Symposium* (201d-204c).

6. St. Angela di Foligno, Italian mystic (1248-1309).

www.ingramcontent.com/pod-product-compliance
Lightning Source LLC
Chambersburg PA
CBHW071137090426
42736CB00012B/2139